All About Plants
ACTIVITY BOOK

by Justine Korman
Illustrations by Cristina Ong

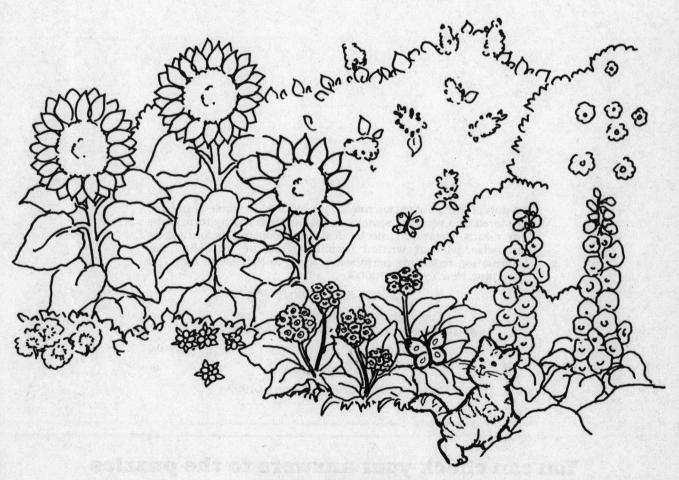

SCHOLASTIC INC.
New York Toronto London Auckland Sydney

ISBN 0-590-47590-8

Copyright © 1993 by Scholastic Inc.
All rights reserved. Published by Scholastic Inc.

24 23 22 21 20 19 18   9/9 0/0

Printed in the U.S.A.   40

First Scholastic printing, August 1993

You can check your answers to the puzzles on pages 31 and 32.

Green Scene

Most plants are green because of a green
chemical that helps them make their own food.
Some plants are not green, though.
Mushrooms are a kind of plant
that is not green.

**Color all the plants on this page green.
Color the rest of the picture
any way you want.**

Small and Tall

Some plants are so small, you can only
see them with a microscope.
Some plants are very big.
The biggest plants on the earth are the giant
sequoia trees of California.
Some sequoias grow more than 310 feet tall!

Circle the tallest plant in each row.

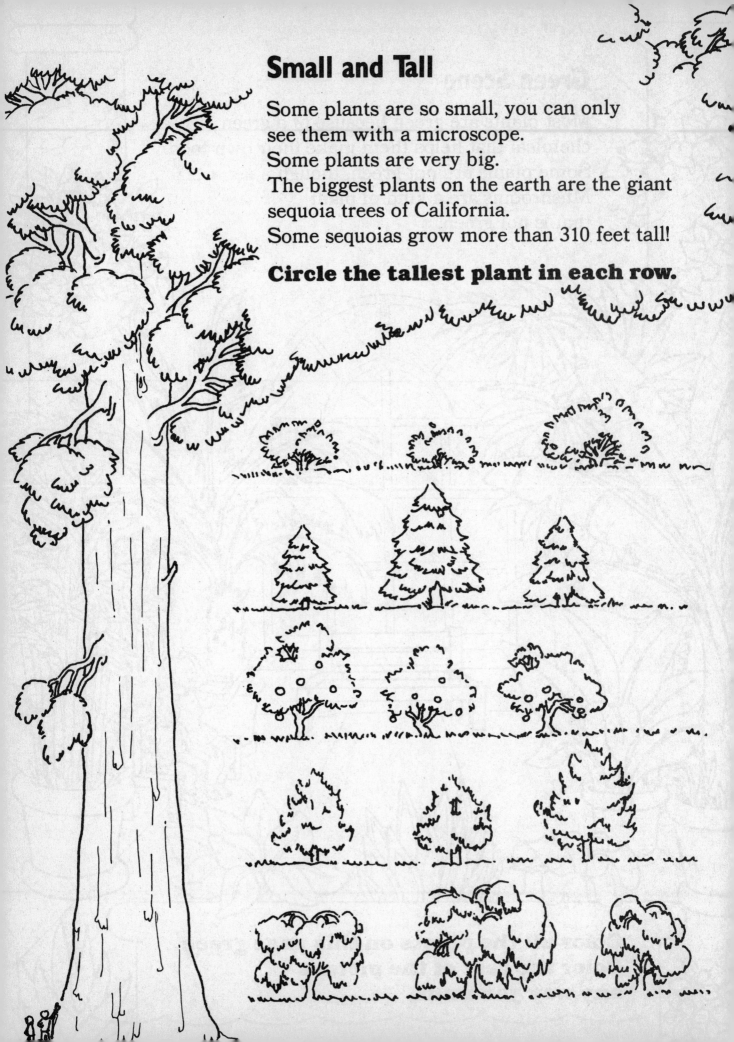

Treats to Eat

Many animals eat plants.
People eat different kinds of fruits,
berries, nuts, and vegetables that come from plants.

Color this page any way you like.

Sun Fun

Plants need sunlight to grow.
Some plants need more sunlight than others.
Smart gardeners know which plants
belong in full sun and which plants
grow well in the shade.

Study this picture carefully.
Then take the memory quiz on the next page.

Sun Fun Memory Quiz

See how many of these questions you can answer correctly without peeking at pages 6 and 7.

1. How many four-legged animals are in the picture? _____
2. Which animal is playing with a butterfly? _____
3. Which animal is burying a bone? _____
4. How many children are in the picture? _____
5. Is someone wearing a hat? _____
6. Who is watering the garden? _____
7. Who is planting seeds? _____
8. Is there a tree in the picture? _____

A Look at Leaves

Leaves collect energy from the sun.
Inside the plant this energy
is used to make food.

Leaves can be many different shapes.

**Complete the leaves on this page.
Draw more leaves if you like.**

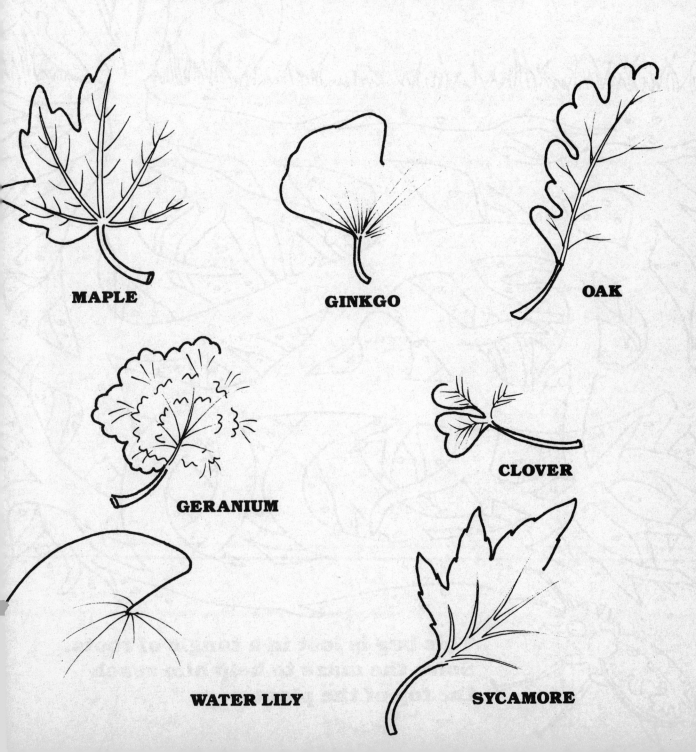

MAPLE

GINKGO

OAK

GERANIUM

CLOVER

WATER LILY

SYCAMORE

Root of the Problem

Plants use their roots to collect water and minerals from the soil.
Roots can be thick or very thin.
Some plants grow roots many yards long in just a few feet of earth.

This bug is lost in a tangle of roots. Solve the maze to help him reach the top of the plant.

Drop by Drop

Plants grow wherever there is sunshine, soil, and rain. Cactus plants grow in deserts where there is very little rain. Cacti store rainwater in their thick branches and trunks. Saguaros are the biggest kind of cactus.

Connect the raindrops from 1 to 25 to see a saguaro cactus.

Sea for Yourself

The first plants on the earth lived in the sea.
Water holds up plants so they don't need stiff stems.
Water also carries minerals needed for growth
and keeps the plants from drying out.

Color all the spaces marked C green to see the name of an underwater plant. Color the rest of the picture any way you like.

Happy Birthday to Tree

Counting the rings inside a stump
will tell you a tree's age.
That's because a tree grows a new layer
(or ring) of wood each year.

**Find the one tree on this page that was
11 years old when it was cut down.**

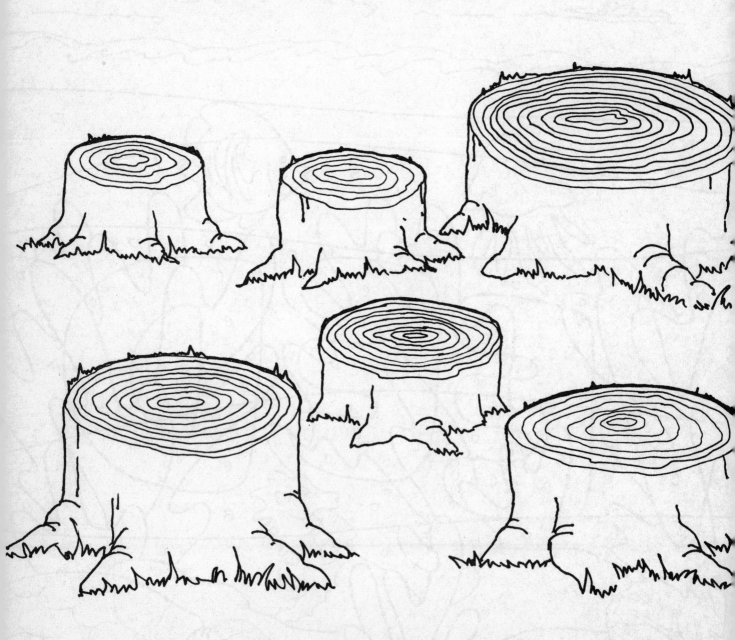

Tricky Tree

In autumn the leaves of many trees change colors and fall. One type of tree stays green through all the seasons.

Use the code to find out the name of this kind of tree. The first letter has been done for you.

E _ _ _ _ _ _ _ _

What Good Is Wood?

Trees have special strong, thick stems that help them grow tall. A tree's single, woody stem is called a trunk.

People use wood from tree trunks to make many things — like the paper for this book!

Find and circle all the things that were made from wood!

Seed Search

A seed contains a baby plant plus food to help it grow.
Some plants cover their seeds with fruit or pods.
Other plants leave their seeds uncovered, sometimes
in cones like pinecones.

**Look across, backwards, up, down, and diagonally
to find the following words: CONE, FLOWER,
FRUIT, GROW, PLANT, POD, SEED.**

```
F R U I T
L D O N N
O T D C A
W S F O L
E E E N P
R E D E T
W O R G D
```

Name Game

Many plants have interesting names.
Some are named after animals.
Tiger lilies are striped like tigers.
Skunk cabbage smells almost as bad as a skunk!

**Ten animals are hiding in this picture.
Use these plant-name clues to find them all:
Cat**tail, **Cranes**bill, **Crow**foot, **Hawk**weed, **Skunk**
cabbage, **Snake** plant, **Spider** plant, **Toad**flax, **Tiger**
lily, Dande**lion. Circle each one as you find it.**

Pollen Page

Many flowers need pollen from other flowers in order to make their seeds. Pollen is the yellow powder at the center of flowers. Pollen floats through the air from one flower to another.

Bees, fruit bats, moths, and hummingbirds also carry pollen from flower to flower.

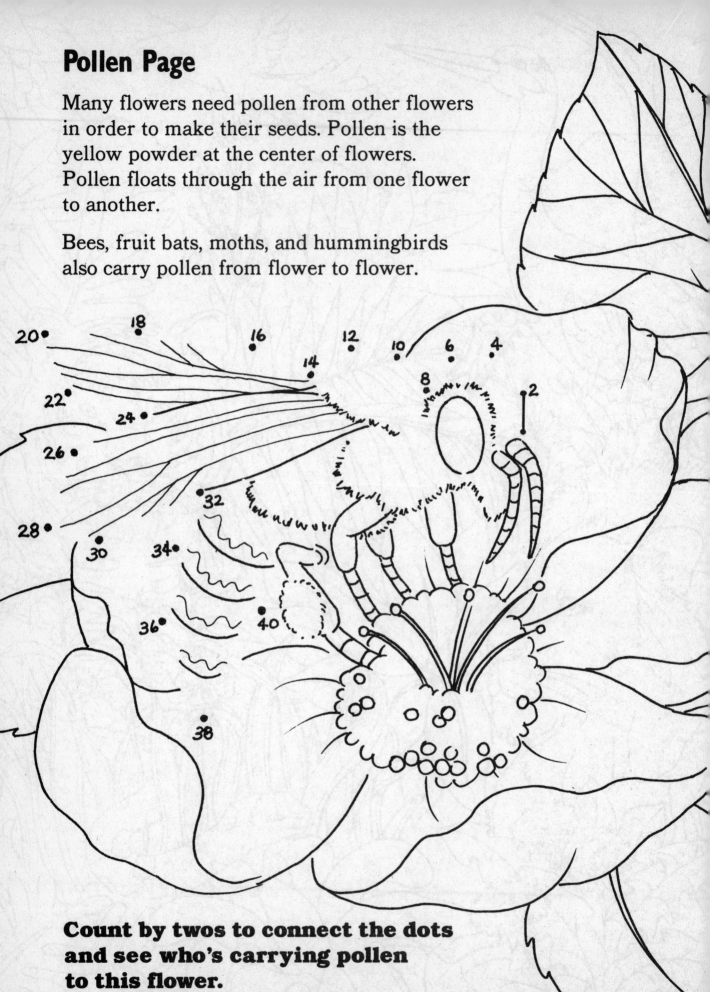

Count by twos to connect the dots and see who's carrying pollen to this flower.

Flower Power

Flowers use bright petals and sweet scents
to attract animals who carry pollen.
Night-flying moths are drawn to white flowers
that glow in the moonlight.
Hummingbirds like red flowers best.

Color all the flowers on this page red.

Wonderful Worms

Bees aren't the only animals who help plants.
Earthworms loosen the soil by crawling through it.
Roots grow better in loose soil. Earthworm
waste adds important minerals to the soil.

When farmers want to know if a field has good
soil, they count earthworms.
The more worms the better!

**How many worms are showing in this
shovelful of soil?**

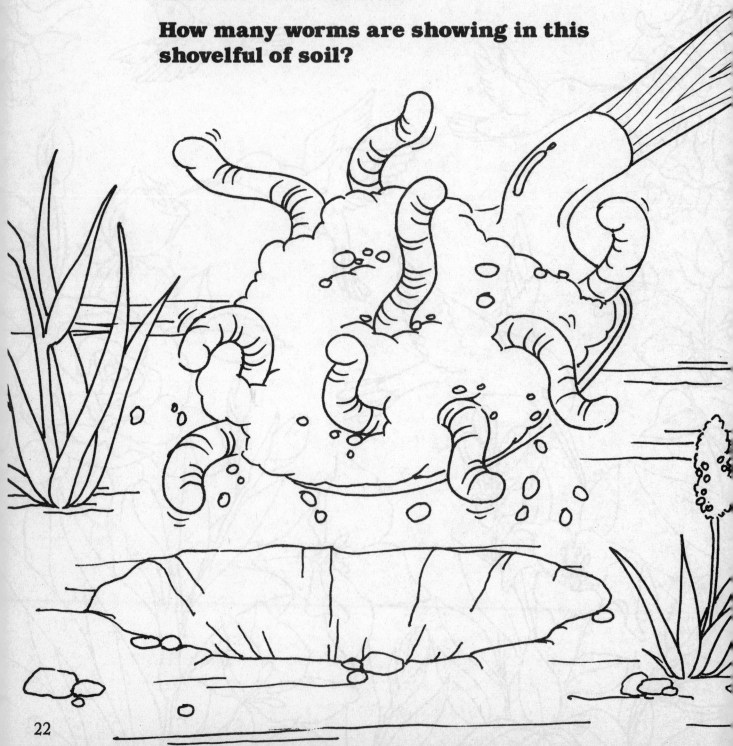

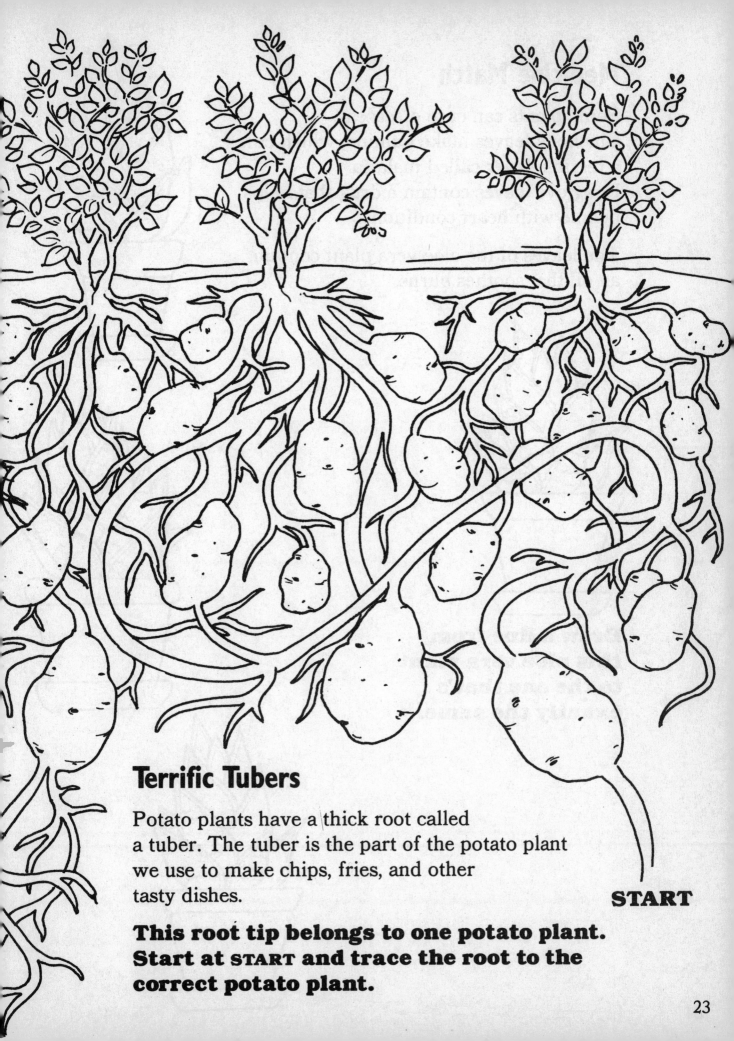

Terrific Tubers

Potato plants have a thick root called
a tuber. The tuber is the part of the potato plant
we use to make chips, fries, and other
tasty dishes.

START

**This root tip belongs to one potato plant.
Start at START and trace the root to the
correct potato plant.**

Medicine Match

Some plants can cure diseases.
Cinchona leaves make quinine, which cures
a terrible fever called malaria.
Foxglove leaves contain a drug that helps
people with heart conditions.

The leaves of the aloe vera plant contain
an oil that soothes burns.

**Draw a line from
this aloe vera plant
to the one that's
exactly the same.**

Good Growing!

Even the biggest tree starts out
as a small seed.
Then the seed sprouts a root and a shoot.
The root grows into the earth.
The shoot reaches up toward the sun.
In time, the shoot becomes a stem
and grows leaves. After many years, that
skinny stem will grow into a mighty trunk.

**These pictures show an oak tree growing
from an acorn. But they are all mixed up!
Write a number from 1 to 6 in the corner of each
picture to show the correct order.**

Frantic Fly

Some plants eat animals.
When an insect lands on a Venus flytrap,
the leaves snap shut.
Over the next two weeks, the plant slowly
digests the soft parts of the insect.
Then the trap opens again.
The insect's shell and wings blow away,
and the trap is ready for its next victim!

**Help this fly escape from the Venus flytraps
by finding the correct route out of the maze.**

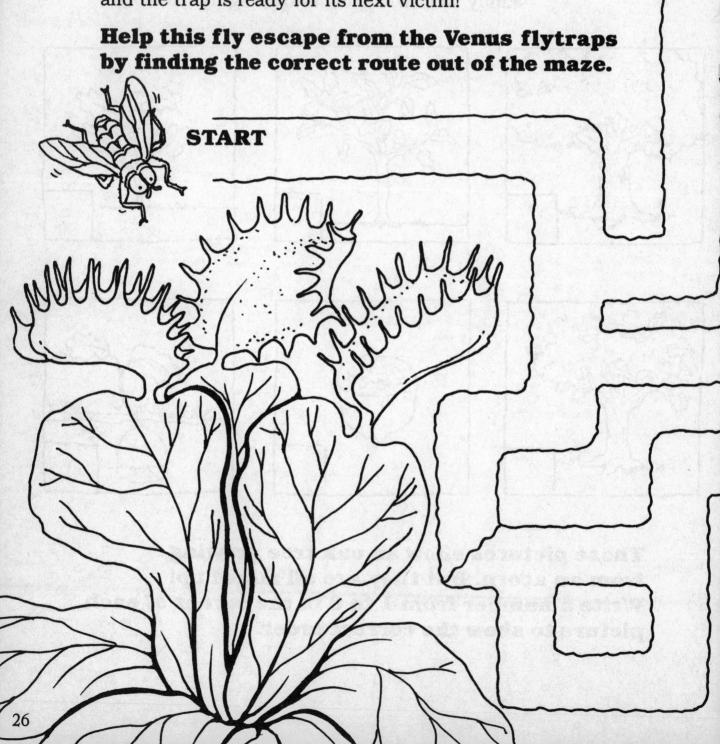

START

FINISH

Moldy Medicine

Did you ever find a bluish-green spot
on a stale piece of bread?
That is a tiny plant called a mold.
People make an important medicine called
penicillin from one kind of mold.

**How many words can you make
from the word PENICILLIN?
We've started the list for you.**

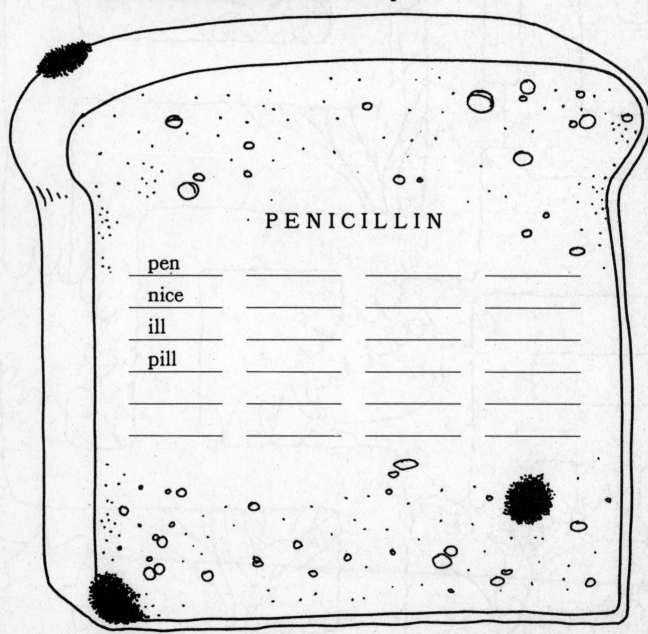

PENICILLIN

pen			
nice			
ill			
pill			

Take a Breather

Animals could not survive without plants.
Plants take in a gas called carbon dioxide
and give off a gas animals and people need to breathe.

**Cross out all the letters that appear more
than once on this tree trunk.
The remaining letters spell the name
of that gas.**

```
A C L O M D
Z D X A D Y
Z G M L C M
E B N B W W
```

Plant Place

There is one place where you can always find plants.
The name of that place is hidden in this roundabout puzzle.
Begin at START, then write every other letter in the puzzle boxes.

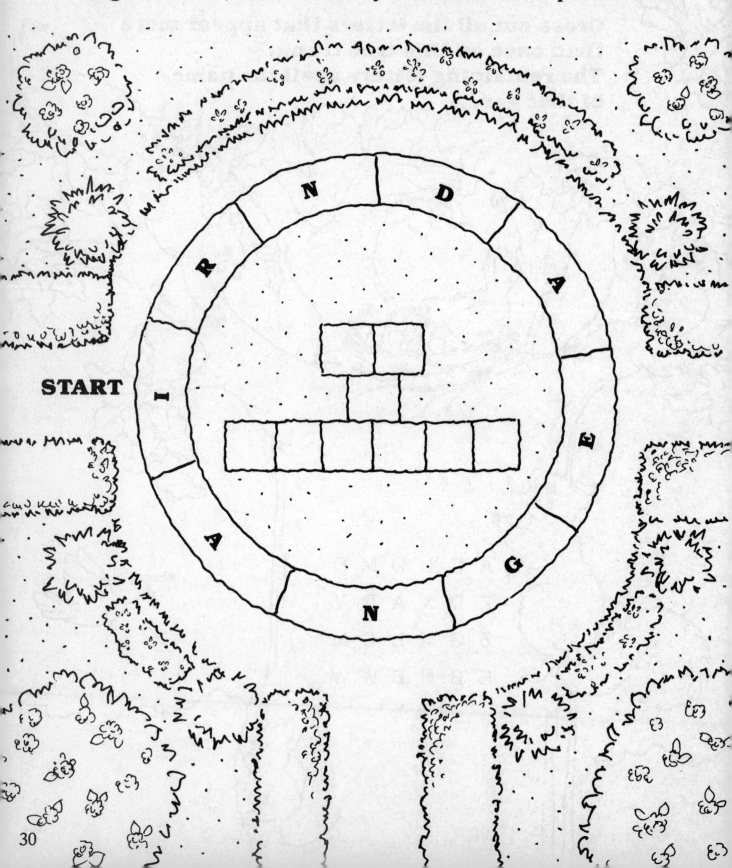

START

Puzzle Answers

Page 4   Small and Tall

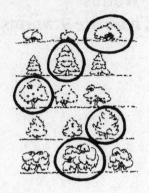

Page 8   Sun Fun
Memory Quiz
1. two
2. the cat
3. the dog
4. two
5. yes
6. the girl
7. the boy
8. yes

Page 10   Root of the Problem

Page 11   Drop by Drop

Pages 12-13   Sea for
Yourself

Page 14   Happy Birthday
to Tree

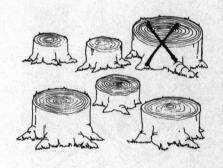

Page 15   Tricky Tree
EVERGREEN

Page 16   What Good Is Wood?

Page 17   Seed Search

Pages 18-19   Name Game

Page 20   Pollen Page

Page 22   Wonderful Worms
There are 9 worms.

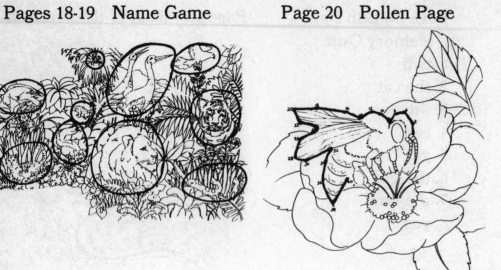

Page 23   Terrific Tubers

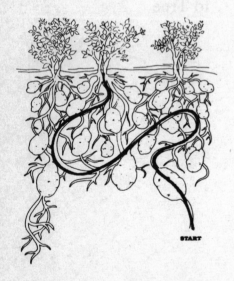

Page 24   Medicine Match

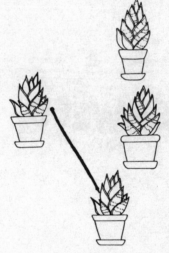

Page 25   Good Growing!

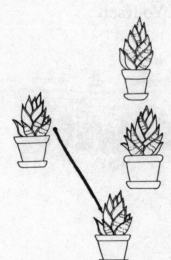

Pages 26-27   Frantic Fly

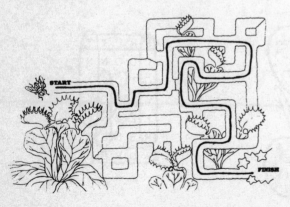

Page 28   Moldy Medicine

ice	inn	Nile	lip	pie
lice	nil	pile	nip	lie
pin	line	cell	Len	Neil
in	pine	clip	pi	lei

Page 29   Take a Breather
OXYGEN

Page 30   Plant Place
IN A GARDEN